BRAVE LEADERS
AND ACTIVISTS

BY J.P. MILLER AND
CHELLIE CARROLL

WAYLAND

A law should never be written to alienate a group or class of people. Yet this has been the plight of black people and other people of colour throughout the world for centuries. Civil rights activists have had to fight for their rights all over the world. These heroes were determined to overturn laws that discriminated against them. They fought to abolish anything that segregated or simply denied equal access to employment, education, medical treatment or public facilities.

In *Black Stories Matter: Brave Leaders and Activists*, you will read the stories of black civil rights activists from around the world. Whether in Africa, the USA, Britain or Australia, their stories run parallel to each other. These are only a few of the men and women who have used their voice to fight for equal treatment and opportunities. It is their feet that paved the way and their shoulders that black people and other people of colour stand upon today.

J.P Miller is a children's book writer who is eager to tell stories about little and well known facts in the African Diaspora. She hopes that her stories will tear down age-long stereotypes and shed light on the many contributions of people of colour throughout the world. J.P lives in Metro Atlanta, Georgia, USA.

Chellie Carroll is an artist from The Dark Peak, who shares her time between her two children, climbing the crags in the Derbyshire hills and producing illustrations that inspire the imagination.

CONTENTS

KOFI ANNAN

THE WEIGHT OF THE WORLD

Becoming a leader meant tackling even bigger world problems but Kofi Annan was ready for it. Growing up in what is now Ghana, his parents taught him that people are never too young to lead. Kofi had worked for the United Nations for 30 years before he became its seventh Secretary General in 1997. He was the first person of African heritage to be elected to that role.

BORN:
8 April 1938 – died 18 August 2018

NATIONALITY:
Ghanaian

OCCUPATION:
Diplomat

Kofi and his twin sister were born in Kumasi, a city in Gold Coast (now Ghana), in 1938. Their father was a businessman and a respected tribal leader who was able to give his four children a good education. Kofi went to university in the USA and Switzerland, and then started work at the United Nations.

Since 1945, the function of the United Nations has been to protect human rights and the environment, promote peace and maintain security for everyone. Kofi looked forward to the challenge.

> "I remain convinced that the only answer to this divided world must be a truly United Nations."

Conflicts often broke out between nations during his time in the job. Some involved a few of the 193 countries that belonged to the United Nations. Then the unthinkable happened on 11 September 2001.

At 8:45 a.m. an American Airlines plane crashed into the North Tower of the World Trade Center in New York, USA, killing all its passengers and crew.

Smoke filled the air and huge chunks of debris fell to the ground. The emergency services rushed to the scene with their sirens blaring. The city was in chaos. At first people thought that the crash was an accident. Then, the unthinkable happened again.

As millions watched the news stories of the first crash, a second passenger plane crashed into the South Tower of the World Trade Center.

Flames burst from the building and another smoke plume rose up into the New York skyline. People started to realise that this was a deliberate act.

In all, four planes crashed that day. One flew into the Pentagon in Washington DC at 9:37 a.m. and the fourth crashed in an open field in Pennsylvania half-an-hour later. Almost 3,000 people died in the attacks.

Kofi, acting as Secretary General of the United Nations, responded passionately to the terrible events:

"There can be no doubt that these attacks are deliberate acts of terrorism, carefully planned and coordinated and as such I condemn them utterly. Terrorism must be fought resolutely wherever it appears."

A resolution was written and passed by the United Nations on 28 September 2011. It stopped member countries from sending aid money to places that might use the money to pay for terrorist acts. It also banned suspected terrorists from travelling, and ordered countries to make careful checks of asylum seekers, to make sure they had no links to terrorist groups. It was among the most radical resolutions that the United Nations has ever considered.

Kofi spent ten years as General Secretary of the United Nations. During this time, he tackled some of the world's biggest problems, including terrorism, poverty and the AIDS crisis. He is remembered for his strong leadership in tackling terrorism but is often criticised for not acting quickly enough to prevent the genocide in Rwanda in the 1990s, when he was head of peacekeeping at the United Nations.

In 2001 Kofi Annan and the United Nations were jointly awarded the Nobel Peace Prize. This recognised Kofi's actions in making the United Nations a stronger organisation and for his work there in protecting human rights.

HARRIET TUBMAN

ESCAPE TO FREEDOM

BORN:
c.1820 – died 10 March 1913

NATIONALITY:
American

OCCUPATION:
Civil rights activist

There was not another soul in sight as Harriet Tubman crossed the state border into Pennsylvania. She had escaped slavery and her life in Maryland, 150 kilometres away. Freedom awaited her on the other side of the Mason Dixon Line, which divided the slave-owning southern states from the free northern states of the USA. Sheer determination pushed Harriet across it.

"When I found I had crossed that line, I looked at my hands to see if I was the same person."

Born into slavery, 27-year-old Harriet had lived in Maryland for her entire life. She stood at the crossroads of her past and her future.

When Harriet looked at her past, she saw her six-year-old self being beaten with a whip for the smallest of things. Harriet had been called 'Minty' back then, short for her birth name, Araminta. She took a new name when she started her new life and changed her name to Harriet, after her mother.

Harriet recalled being made to crawl through the thick mud of the Little Black River to hunt muskrats when she was just a

child. She remembered when, at the age of 12, she stepped between an angry plantation overseer and the slave he was about to hit with a heavy metal weight. The weight landed on Harriet's head instead, leaving her with lifelong injuries. She thought about the marriage she had left behind.

When Harriet looked into the future, she saw freedom and opportunity. But sadness tugged at her heart. Her brothers were supposed to have been there beside her. All three had tried to escape once before, but her brothers had turned back. This time, Harriet had set off alone.

Every winter after her escape, Harriet braved the journey back to Maryland to bring her family members to freedom too. She eventually freed her brothers and both her parents, and any other slaves who wanted to escape. She used a network of secret stops and led slaves along hidden trails called the Underground Railroad. They found freedom at first in Pennsylvania but, after the Fugitive Slave Act of 1850 was passed, Pennsylvania was too dangerous. Harriet had to add another 650 kilometres to the journey to reach freedom in Canada.

There were other guides on the Underground Railroad, but Harriet Tubman was one of the best. For 11 years Harriet walked thousands of kilometres and personally rescued hundreds of people from slavery. During that time she outwitted many enslavers and the bounty-hunters they paid to try to capture her.

Because she led her people to freedom, Harriet earned the nickname 'Black Moses' after the biblical leader, Moses, who led his people to freedom from slavery in Egypt. Harriet prided herself on two things:

"I was a conductor on the Underground Railroad for over eight years ... I never ran my train off the track and I never lost a passenger."

The news of Harriet's courage and daring travelled. When the American Civil War broke out in 1861 between the northern and the southern states of America, Harriet joined the northern Union Army. She became the first African-American woman to plan and lead a raid, helping to free hundreds of slaves.

In later life Harriet found new causes to fight for. She spoke out for women to have the right to vote and travelled around the country to gather support for this cause. She remarried and lived in Auburn, New York, where she died and was buried in 1913.

LOWITJA O'DONOGHUE

BEATING THE ODDS

A difficult childhood can be a lifelong burden for some. Not Lowitja O'Donoghue. She was determined to beat the odds and rise above her early experiences in order to improve the lives of Aboriginal Australian communities.

BORN:
1 August 1932

NATIONALITY:
Australian/Aboriginal Australian

OCCUPATION:
Nurse and campaigner

The daughter of an Irish–Australian father and an Aboriginal–Australian mother, Lowitja was taken away from her mother at the age of two by the Australian government. She was put into the care of missionaries at Colebrook Home near Quorn.

Lowitja was one of over 100,000 children with Aboriginal Australian backgrounds who were separated from their families between about 1900 and 1970, to become part of 'The Stolen Generation'.

At Colebrook Home the missionaries tried to strip Lowitja of her Aboriginal language, beliefs and identity in favour of her white heritage from the father she never

knew. They even changed her name to Lois. Lowitja O'Donoghue did not see her mother for over thirty years.

> "I always thought about what my mother was feeling, whether she cared or if she ever asked where her children might be."

No one ever answered Lowitja's questions about her mother or her family. She left Colebrook Home at the age of 16 to go to high school in Adelaide. Lowitja wanted to be a nurse. She enjoyed caring for people and had already helped to look after the children at the home.

The Royal Adelaide Hospital was accepting applications for their nurse training course. Lowitja applied, but was turned down because of her Aboriginal Australian background. "Go back to the place where you belong," she was told.

But that just made Lowitja more determined. She applied many more times. Finally, she was accepted. In 1954 Lowitja became the first Aboriginal Australian nurse in South Australia.

After working as a nurse for a year in India, Lowitja returned to Australia. She worked as a nurse and a welfare officer in remote parts of South Australia where she became known as a skilled campaigner for better rights for Aboriginal Australian people.

It was during this time that Lowitja was finally reunited with her mother. While working in the remote town of Coober Pedy, Lowitja's aunt and uncle saw her in a supermarket and spotted the family likeness. Her mother was living in the nearby town of Oodnadatta and the two met again, after 33 years apart.

Lowitja O'Donoghue continued to fight to improve the lives of Aboriginal Australian and Torres Strait Islander people in Australia. Her work helped in the creation of new laws that established the rights of Aboriginal Australians and Torres Strait Islanders to own land and water.

Lowitja was named Australian of the Year in 1984 and has received several other awards. She regularly wears the red, black and yellow colours of the Aboriginal Australian flag with pride when she accepts awards and attends ceremonies. In 1993, Lowitja became the first Aboriginal Australian person to address the United Nations General Assembly.

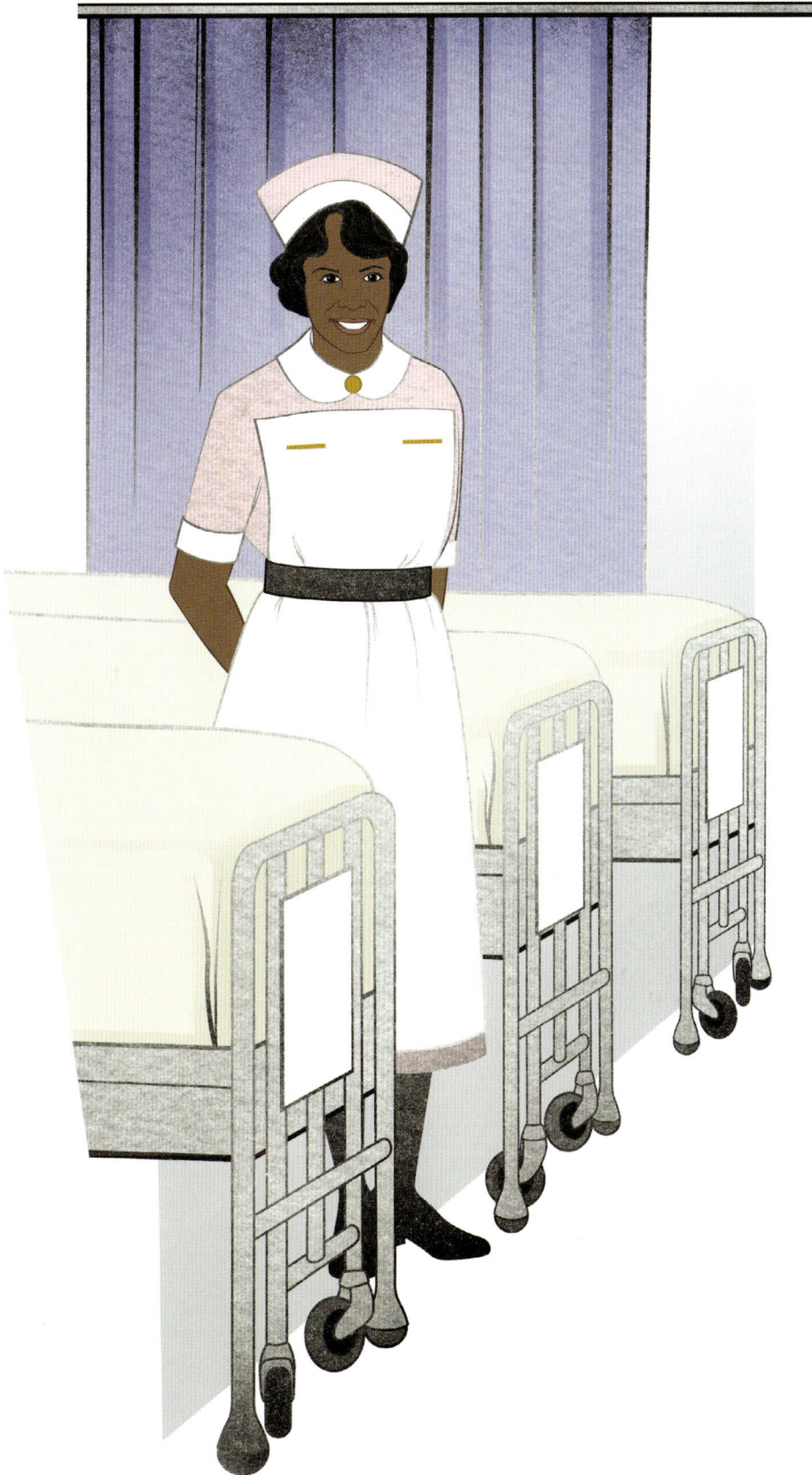

NELSON MANDELA

THE PEOPLE'S HERO

BORN: 18 July 1918 – died 5 December 2013

NATIONALITY: South African

OCCUPATION: Lawyer, activist and politician

Black people in South Africa were suffering. They were being removed from their homes and forced to live separately from white people under the laws known as apartheid. To travel from one place to another, they had to carry passbooks. Some were stripped of their citizenship and could no longer vote.

Black South Africa needed a leader – a leader that would take command and lead them to freedom. Such a leader emerged. His name? Nelson Mandela.

Born Rolihlahla Mandela, the son of a Thembu chief, his teacher gave him the nickname 'Nelson' on his first day at school. After his father died when Nelson was only 12 years old, his uncle took him into his home and brought him up alongside his own son. Nelson went to good schools and on to university, and eventually became a lawyer.

From his university days onwards, Nelson became interested in politics. He worked closely with the African National Congress (ANC), an organisation working for better rights for black South Africans through non-violent protest.

ANC supporters deliberately entered whites-only hospitals, towns and government buildings to protest against apartheid laws, which kept black and white South Africans apart and treated black people very unfairly.

In 1960, a protest in Sharpeville against the unfair passbook laws took an ugly turn. Unarmed protestors were killed by the police. The South African government declared a state of emergency and the ANC was banned from organising any further protests. Nelson started to think that non-violent protests were not working.

"There are many people who feel that it is useless and futile to continue talking about peace and non-violence against a government whose only reply is savage attacks on an unarmed and defenceless people."

The military wing of the ANC took shape under Nelson's leadership. Blacks of South Africa were standing up to the attacks against them with bomb attacks on government targets.

Nelson travelled secretly across Africa to gain support from other countries, disguised as a driver, a chef or a gardener to avoid detection. He commanded troops for over a year and planned damaging attacks on water works and power stations. With each success, Nelson gained popularity and respect. Black South Africans were confident he was leading them to freedom.

This hope was dashed when Nelson was captured at a police roadblock in Durban one night. In 1964 he was sentenced to life in prison for conspiring to overthrow the government.

Prison life was harsh. The days were filled with breaking rocks or sewing sacks. Members of Nelson's family died while he was in prison but he was not allowed to go to their funerals.

As word spread about his imprisonment, Nelson gained support from people all over the world. At home in South Africa, the anti-apartheid movement grew and grew and he came to be seen as its natural leader, much to the embarrassment of the South African government.

After 27 years in prison, Nelson Mandela walked free in 1990, at the age of 71. Almost immediately he started to lead the African National Congress again and work for equal rights for all South Africans. Three years later, in 1993, he was awarded the Nobel Peace Prize for his work against apartheid. A year later he became the first black President of South Africa after South Africa's first election in which all South Africans could vote.

"We shall build a society in which all South Africans, both black and white, will be able to walk tall without any fear in their hearts, assured of the inalienable right to human dignity, a rainbow nation at peace with itself and the world."

UMRA OMAR

A SENSE OF RESPONSIBILITY

The boat engine hummed as the boat splashed through the waves of the Indian Ocean. It would be home for Umra Omar and her crew for the next three days. They were on their monthly journey to the Lamu islands, off the coast of Kenya, to deliver free medical care.

BORN: 15 June 1983

NATIONALITY: Kenyan

OCCUPATION: Founder of Safari Doctors and conservationist

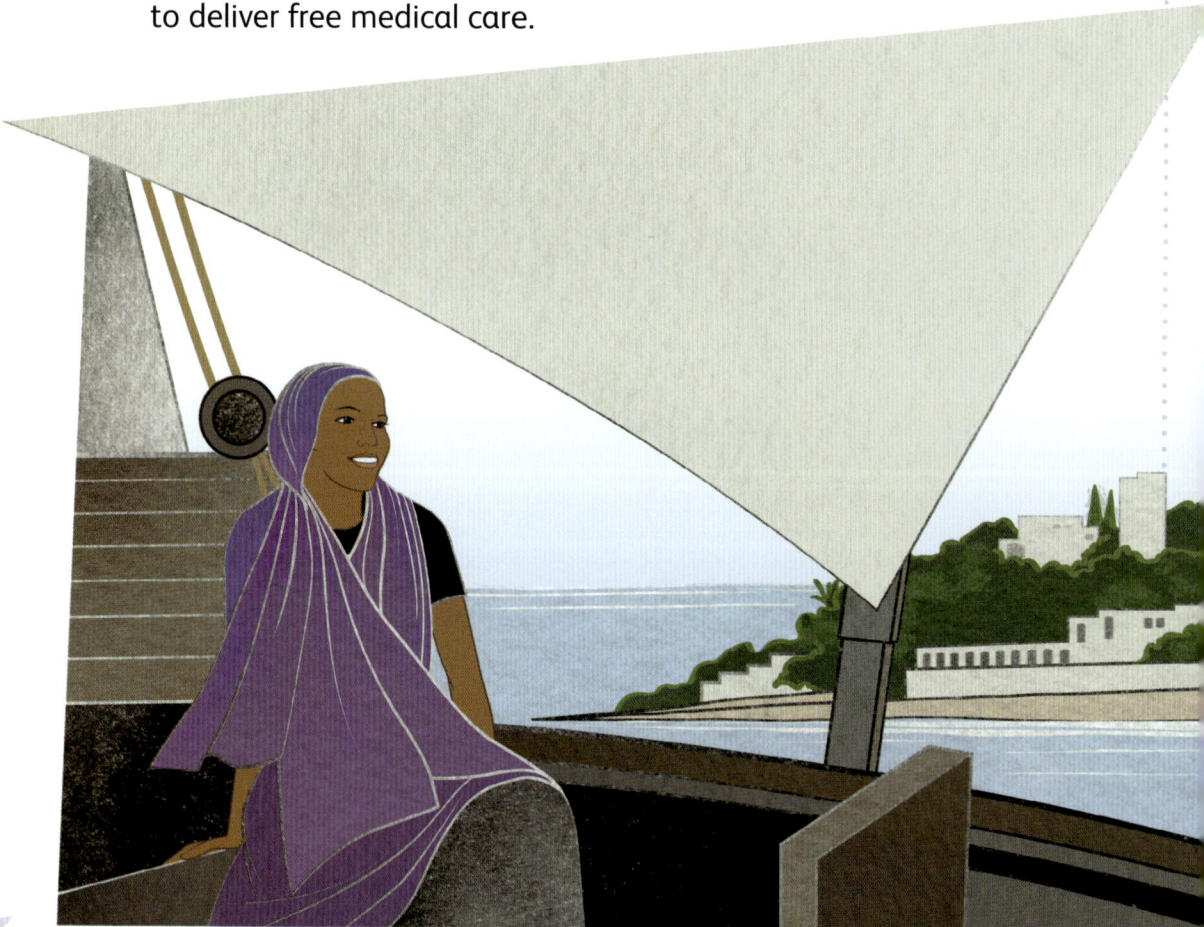

Umra gazed across the blue sea at the sandy beaches of the island of Kiangwe. After she'd studied for university degrees in the USA, she had found work in Washington DC. But Umra felt she had important work to do in Africa, so she had returned home to Kenya. Months later, in 2015, she founded Safari Doctors, an organisation offering free medical care to the people of the Lamu islands. It was something Umar felt she had to do.

"It was ... a sense of responsibility."

Umra was born in Mombasa, but spent her early childhood on Pate Island, one of the Lamu islands. Here her grandmother looked after Umra and her sister while their mother completed her studies abroad. The Lamu islands were once busy tourist destinations. Then they were attacked by the Islamic terrorist group, Al-Shabaab.

When the unrest began, the group that had previously provided medical care on the islands closed their clinics. They fled the islands, leaving six of the ten villages with no healthcare.

Not long after, Umra's Safari Doctors dropped anchor close to the fishing village of Kiangwe. She and the crew were met with smiling faces and helping hands.

Because of the conflict, Kiangwe primary school had been closed and was turned into a Kenyan army base, to keep the islanders safe. The Safari Doctors used part of the school to set up clinics when they made visits to the village.

One schoolroom was a clinic caring for mothers and babies. A second room was used for appointments with a volunteer doctor. Another was a makeshift pharmacy.

To this day, the volunteers and staff who work for Safari Doctors travel by boat, plane and motorcycle to treat over 1,000 patients a month.

"We put together a trip for Safari Doctors like we would a thousand-piece puzzle."

Putting those pieces together is something Umra does very well. From the government to local fishemen, she uses every resource available.

Together they ensure that these island people have access to good medical care.

Since founding Safari Doctors in 2015, Umra has been named one of Cable News Network's (CNN's) Top 10 Heroes in 2016. She was given the United Nations in Kenya Person of the Year Award in 2017. She continues to work for Safari Doctors and also is involved with conservation projects along the coast of Kenya.

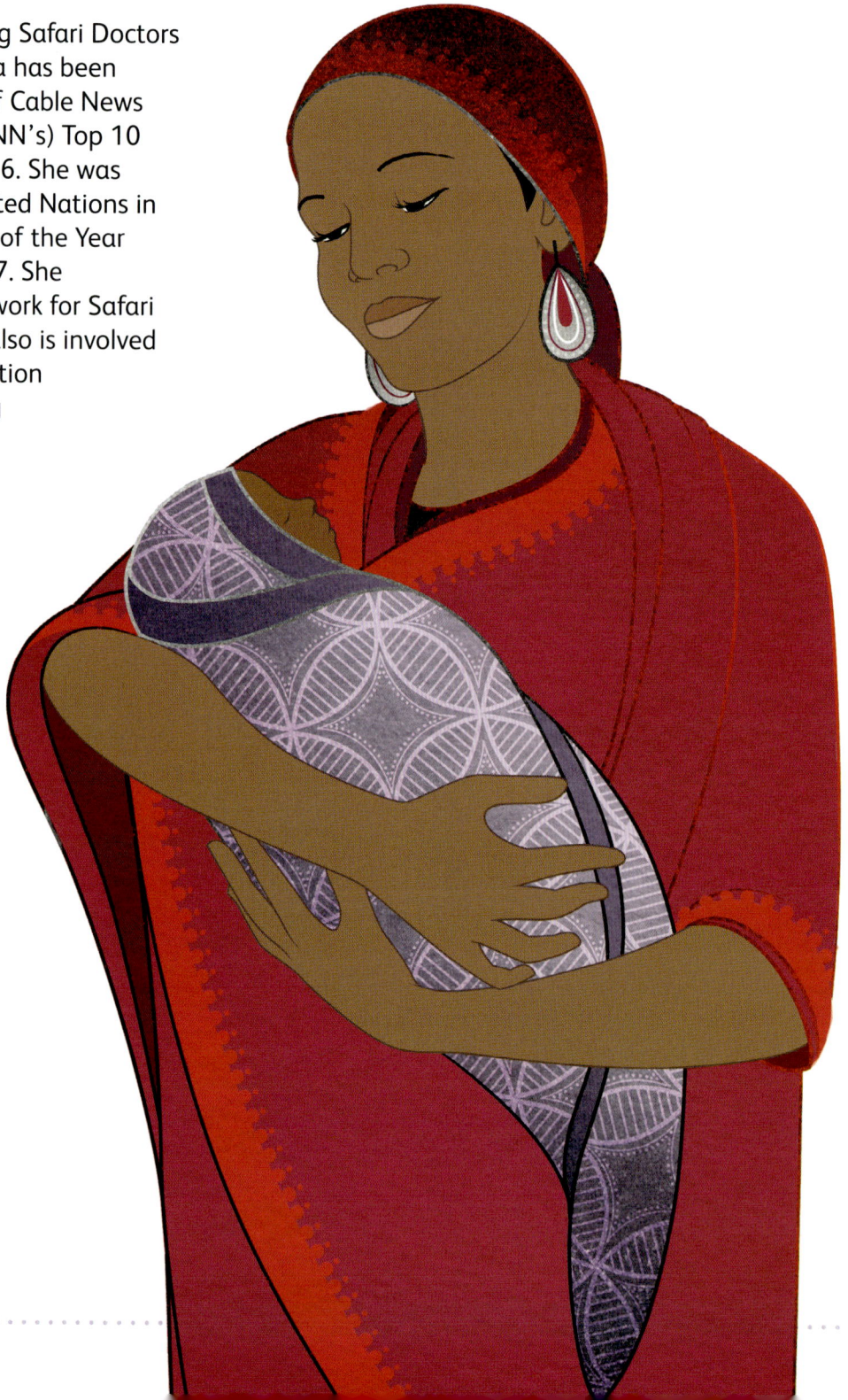

ALICIA GARZA, PATRISSE CULLORS AND OPAL TOMETI

#BLACKLIVESMATTER

BORN:
Garza (1981), Cullors (1984), Tometi (1984)

NATIONALITY:
American

OCCUPATION:
Human rights activists

In 2013, the heart of black America skipped a beat. For over a year, since the senseless killing of unarmed teenager, Trayvon Martin, black Americans had believed that his killer would go to prison. Then the judge's verdict was read out: NOT GUILTY.

Immediately, people turned to social media. They tried to make sense of what had just happened. Writer and activist Alicia Garza wrote a post on her Facebook page: 'Black people. I love you. I love us. Our lives matter.' Her friend, Patrisse Cullors, added the hashtag:

#BlackLivesMatter

Within minutes the hashtag went viral, bringing national attention to the violence and police brutality towards black people in America. It became the rallying cry at protests and rallies all over the country. Community activist Opal Tometi was determined to join Alicia and Patrisse in making Black Lives Matter an important movement. She saw it as a new vision for blacks around the world, and a call to action for equal human rights for blacks and whites.

Two years after the Black Lives Matter movement began, Eric Garner, an African-American man, was choked to death by police in Staten Island, New York, while they were arresting him for supposedly selling cigarettes illegally. Not even a month later, another unarmed black teenager, Michael Brown, was shot dead by a white police officer in Ferguson, Missouri. Outrage at this death made thousands of people gather in protest in Ferguson and around the USA. Patrisse remembers that protestors found themselves face to face with heavily-armed police officers.

The Black Lives Matter movement was back in the national news. The battle cry of "Hands up! Don't shoot!" rang out at protest rallies and demonstrations across the nation. Protestors walked along main roads, bringing traffic to a halt. Five St Louis Rams footballers raised their hands in the 'hands up' gesture in support of the movement during a match. Elsewhere, LeBron James warmed up for a National Basketball Association game wearing a T-shirt printed with the words 'I Can't Breathe!' to remind people of Eric Garner's death at the hands of the police. Black Lives Matter was picking up steam.

The Black Lives Matter movement was not popular with everyone. Some news outlets began to spread fear that its founders encouraged hate and harm against the US police force. A counter-movement was established in 2014 – Blue Lives Matter. It aimed to support police officers who faced negative news coverage of their actions, and to remind people of the dangers that police officers face every day.

The Black Lives Matter founders, Alicia, Patrisse and Opal, spoke out in response: "We are not a movement about harming police – but a movement about holding the police accountable."

Black Lives Matter began as a social media sensation but has grown into a national, and international, protest movement, campaigning for fairer treatment of black people not just by the police but in all areas of their lives. In 2017, the Black Lives Matter founders, Alicia, Patrisse and Opal, were presented with the Sydney Peace Prize.

ROSA PARKS

THE BUS JOURNEY THAT CHANGED THE USA

BORN: 4 February 1913 – died 24 October 2005

NATIONALITY: American

OCCUPATION: Civil rights activist

The bus was already crowded with people travelling home after a long day's work. Rosa Parks paid her fare and scanned the Colored Only section with her eyes. Luckily there was an empty seat just behind the Whites Only section.

This was 1950s America where laws separated black and white Americans on the bus, in the cinema, sent them to separate schools and made them play in separate playgrounds. The bus travelled along the streets of Montgomery, Alabama, stopping to let people off and allow others to board.

Soon the bus was full. The bus driver turned around and ordered the black people on board to give up their 'Colored Only' seats to white passengers. Three black people sitting near Rosa reluctantly did so. But not Rosa.

The bus driver looked Rosa straight in the face and asked if she was going to stand.
"I am not!" she said.
"I'll have you arrested!"
"You may do that!"

7053

By the time the police arrived, many of the black passengers had got off the bus and walked home. They didn't want any trouble.

"Did the driver tell you to stand?" the police officer asked Rosa.
"Yes."
"Why didn't you stand?"
"I don't think that I should have to stand. Why do you push us around?"
"I don't know, but the law is the law and you're under arrest."

Rosa was taken to the police station. She was photographed, fingerprinted and charged with breaking Chapter 6, Section 11 of the Montgomery City Code – the vacant seat provision. But she never regretted her decision, even though it ultimately cost both Rosa and her husband their jobs.

"I was tired, but not physically tired. I had made up my mind that I would not give in any longer to legally enforced segregation."

Rosa had inherited her courage and desire for justice from her mother and grandparents. They believed in the fair and equal treatment of all people. Rosa wanted the same, as did her husband. They had been active members of the National Association for the Advancement of Colored People (NAACP) for many years. Rosa had travelled around Alabama, interviewing victims of racism. She recorded the stories of those who had witnessed lynchings or beatings.

In protest at Rosa's arrest, the black citizens of Montgomery took part in a boycott of public buses led by the powerful activist Martin Luther King (see pages 29–34). The boycott continued for 381 days. The buses stood empty as black people shared cars, used taxis driven by African Americans or simply walked.

The boycott was a huge success. On 13 November 1956 the US Supreme Court ruled that segregation on public transport was against the law.

Rosa Parks had proved that she, and black African Americans everywhere, were not going to be pushed around anymore.

DR MARTIN LUTHER KING, JR

TWO OPPOSITES: ONE GOAL

The peaceful protests against segregation in Birmingham, Alabama, USA began in April 1963, with African Americans holding sit-ins and marches, and boycotting local shops. At the heart of the protests was the charismatic clergyman and civil rights leader, Dr Martin Luther King, Jr.

BORN:
15 January 1929 – died 4 April 1968

COUNTRY:
American

OCCUPATION:
Clergyman and civil rights activist

Martin was one of the most famous faces of the US civil rights movement. During the early days of the Birmingham protests, he was arrested for breaking a law against public protest, and put in prison. But the protests continued. On 2 May, over a thousand local students and schoolchildren joined the movement. The police were determined to halt the protests, so they turned high-pressure water hoses on the crowd.

They also unleashed their fierce police dogs. Police arrested over 4,000 protesters. Photos and films of the brutal scenes made headline news in the USA.

The violent events prompted the US President John F Kennedy to take action, saying:

"...The events in Birmingham and elsewhere have increased the cries for equality. No city, or state or legislative body can prudently choose to ignore them."

It was the attention and the reaction that Martin had hoped the Birmingham campaign would bring. Just three months later he was in the country's capital city, Washington, DC, making his most famous 'I have a dream' speech to an audience of over 250,000 people. The road to civil rights reform had just made a crucial turn.

A year later Martin was awarded the Nobel Peace Prize and US President Johnson signed a law that outlawed all racial discrimination. Martin set out to continue his life's work, but some people wanted to silence him. In 1968 he was tragically assassinated.

MALCOLM X

TWO OPPOSITES: ONE GOAL

News travelled fast. On 14 April 1957 the New York police had badly beaten Johnson Hinton, a member of the Nation of Islam. An angry crowd gathered outside the police station where the injured man was being held. To help calm the situation down, the police allowed Malcolm X, a Nation of Islam minister, to see Johnson. Once they had agreed to get medical attention for Johnson, Malcolm agreed to help the police.

Malcolm raised his hand. To the amazement of the police, the crowd dispersed and went home.

"Did you see what I just saw?" one asked the other. "That is too much power for one [black] man to have!"

The incident won Malcolm X new fame. After a difficult childhood, Malcolm had turned to crime in his youth and spent time in prison for burglary. While he was there, his brother visited him and told him about the Nation of Islam, a movement which combined the teachings of Islam with black nationalism.

After he was released from prison, Malcolm quickly rose to the top of the movement, second in command to its founder, Elijah Muhammad. Malcolm's intelligence, passion and charisma made him a powerful leader in the US black civil rights movement.

Dr Martin Luther King and Malcolm X were very different men and had very different beliefs. Martin was a Christian clergyman with a strong belief that peaceful protest would lead to blacks and whites working together to build a better world.

Malcolm X believed in action of any kind, including violence, and, according to the teachings of the Nation of Islam, felt that white people took away black people's confidence and influence in the world. He changed his surname from 'Little' to 'X' as he saw 'Little' as the name given to his ancestors by their slave owners. He even believed that black people should live in their own separate country, separated from white people, although he may have changed this view later in his life.

Martin Luther King and Malcolm X shared a common goal though: to end the unfair treatment of black people by white people because of the colour of their skin.

These two very different, but inspirational, leaders met for the first and only time in Washington D.C. in March 1964. Many took their handshake afterwards as an act of friendship. Their shared goal of equal rights for black people was in sight.

The Civil Rights Act of 1964 was signed by US president, Lyndon B Johnson, on 2 July 1964. That same year, Malcolm split from the Nation of Islam as a result of a disagreement with its leader. Less than a year later, Malcolm X was assassinated in Harlem, New York, on 21 February 1965 by three Nation of Islam followers. Three years later, Dr Martin Luther King was shot dead by a racist criminal in Memphis, Tennessee on 4 April 1968.

STUART HALL

WHO ARE WE AND WHERE DO WE BELONG?

What happens when one group of people controls another in the same society? As a student at Oxford University and, later, as a university lecturer, Stuart Hall discussed this question and many others. He wanted to help people understand who they are by thinking about what it means to be British, especially if you come from an immigrant background.

BORN:
3 February 1932 – died 10 February 2014

COUNTRY:
Jamaican–British

OCCUPATION:
Academic, cultural theorist

Stuart dedicated his life to researching the answer to that and other questions. He wanted to help others understand the power of the dominant culture of a society and the way it influences others.

Stuart studied the way black people in particular made sense of their place in British life, its culture and society at a time when most British people felt that to be British, you had to have white skin.
This white dominant culture continued despite the fact that from the 1950s onwards, huge numbers of British citizens from Britain's colonies in the Caribbean, India and elsewhere, came to Britain to work or to study.

> ## "Culture is the way we make sense of, or give meaning to the world."

Stuart was born in 1932 in Kingston, Jamaica, which at that time was still part of the British Empire. He went to good schools where he received a British education. His mother thought that Britain and Britishness were best, an idea that Stuart found increasingly difficult as he grew up.

Stuart won a scholarship to study English literature at the University of Oxford. He enjoyed university but he was at a crossroads. Now he felt like an outsider in Jamaica and in Britain. It was about this time that Stuart began to form his own thoughts about culture. He believed that the ways in which different countries won power varied, but the ways they kept that power were the same. They, the dominant country and its government, managed to persuade the people of the countries they had taken over to accept the dominant country's beliefs and values.

The longer Stuart lived in Britain, the more attached he became to his blackness, and all that it meant to him.

After university he became a teacher and then moved to Birmingham, where he became head of cultural studies at Birmingham University. He worked on many research papers with his students, exploring different areas of multicultural life in Britain before moving on to become a professor of sociology at the Open University. He presented many television programmes exploring his ideas about culture, and the ways that black British people were influencing and becoming part of British culture.

Stuart died in 2014 at the age of 82. Without his pioneering work, books like this one about black lives might never have been written.

BARACK OBAMA

HIS STORY

BORN: 4 August 1961

NATIONALITY:
American

OCCUPATION:
Politician and lawyer

The air was bone-chillingly cold. Usually, people did not stay outdoors for long in such low temperatures. But this was not an ordinary day in Washington, DC, the capital of the USA. It was Tuesday, 20 January 2009 and Barack Hussein Obama was about to be sworn in as the 44th president of the USA.

After studying law at university, Barack became a civil rights lawyer but moved into politics when he was elected to the Illinois State Senate in 1997, then the US Senate in 2004. In the keynote speech at the 2004 Democratic Convention, he spoke movingly of his parents who had met in university and, despite a complicated family life, had instilled in him the values of generosity and tolerance.

Barack became a leader whom people respected and admired. Whether he was a community organiser fighting for people's rights or he was setting up a job training programme, people trusted the young Harvard Law School graduate. Their trust led him all the way to the White House, home to the US president.

"In no other country on Earth is my story even possible."

Now over a million supporters had packed themselves into the Washington Mall to witness the historic moment when Barack became president. The nation had elected its first African American president. For older African Americans it was a victory they had hardly dared to dream of during their lifetime.

If Barack was nervous, you couldn't tell. He laid his left hand on the Bible held by his wife Michelle, a Bible that had once belonged to President Abraham Lincoln (president from 1861–65). As his daughters, Malia and Sasha, proudly looked on, Barack Obama raised his right hand and was sworn in as US president.

In his first hundred days in office, President Obama ordered the withdrawal of US military troops from Iraq. He signed the Lilly Ledbetter Fair Pay Act that aimed to pay people of whichever sex fairly for their work. And, staying true to a campaign promise, President Obama brought in a huge spending plan to save jobs and create new ones where possible.

President Obama will best be remembered as the president with a warm heart. In 2009, he was awarded the Nobel Peace Prize for his work in international diplomacy and, in particular, his efforts to persuade countries to lay down their nuclear weapons.

Barack also protected wild areas and their wildlife and took action against climate change. He will also be remembered as a president who fought for better healthcare for all US citizens, saying:

"We are the only advanced democracy on Earth – the only wealthy nation – that allows such hardships for millions of its people."

In 2012, Barack Obama was re-elected for a second term as president until January 2017 but his story is not yet finished. Barack is now an author and a popular public speaker, donating much of the proceeds from their work to his and his wife Michelle's charitable foundations.

Read on to find out about some other amazing black leaders and activists, both past and present.

AKON

Akon lights Africa! The bestselling singer is on a mission to bring solar electricity to rural Africa. Every major African city has electricity, but many rural communities are completely in the dark.

Akon, whose real name is Aliaune Damala Badara Akon Thiam, was born in the US, but spent his early years in Senegal, in a home with no electricity or running water. Years later, he begged his grandmother to let him install electricity at her home. She refused. Akon decided that if she wouldn't allow him to bring electricity to her, he would do it by providing electricity to all of Africa instead!

With the help of funding from China, Akon's project has supplied solar power to rural people in 14 African countries, installing over 100,000 streetlights and 1,000 micro-generators. He has also set up a training school in Mali where young people gain the skills needed to roll out this solar power project. He has brought light and power to millions of Africans.

BORN:
16 April 1973

NATIONALITY:
Senegalese–American

OCCUPATION:
Musician, actor, philanthropist

DIANE ABBOTT

BORN:
27 September 1953

NATIONALITY:
British

OCCUPATION:
Politician

Diane Abbott has been a Member of Parliament (MP) in Britain for over twenty years. First elected in 1987, she became the first ever black woman MP. To mark this fact, the Houses of Parliament paid for a portrait to be painted of her.

Diane is perhaps best known for her campaign to highlight the challenges that face black schoolchildren in London and the rest of the UK. The organisation she founded holds workshops and conferences to help parents, teachers and everyone else improve opportunities for black students. Diane is also a passionate champion of human rights.

NEVILLE BONNER

It was August 1971. The day had finally arrived for Neville Bonner to be sworn into the Australian Parliament. It was an exciting moment for Australia's Aboriginal community. Soon, one of them would be the first Aboriginal Australian to become a senator. During the ceremony, Neville heard the voice of his grandfather: "It's all right now boy, you are finally in the council of your Australian elders." But the real work was about to begin.

BORN:
28 March 1922 – died
5 February 1999

COUNTRY:
Australian

OCCUPATION:
Politician

Neville used his political position to help Aboriginal Australians be recognised and respected as responsible citizens. He worked with the One People of Australia League (OPAL) to improve the lives of Aboriginal Australians, their housing, education and life chances, and to protect their land rights. In 1979, Neville was jointly named Australian of the Year.

KIMBERLY BRYANT

Kimberly Bryant was already a well-respected electrical engineer by the time her 12-year-old daughter, Kia, expressed an interest in computer science. Eager to help her daughter discover it for herself, Kimberly enrolled Kia in a computer summer school. Kia was keen to learn but she soon realised that the girls didn't get as much attention as the boys. Each day Kia told her mother how the teacher nearly always picked the boys to answer questions. Kimberly did not want her daughter to become unmotivated or to feel like she couldn't learn the skills.

So Kimberly founded Black Girls Code. The organisation introduces girls from non-white backgrounds to computer programming through after-school and summer schools. The organisation has grown and even holds classes in South Africa. Its aim is to give one million girls the skills they need to work in computing by 2050.

BORN:
14 January 1967

NATIONALITY:
American

OCCUPATION:
Engineer

CRAIG WATKINS

BORN:
16 November 1967

NATIONALITY:
American

OCCUPATION:
Lawyer

The United Nation's Universal Declaration of Human Rights declares that everyone accused of a crime is innocent until proven guilty. But what happens when the accused is innocent and is still sent to prison?

Dallas County, Texas, USA had one of the highest crime rates in the USA when District Attorney (lawyer) Craig Watkins took office in 2006. The county had also sent more innocent people to prison than any other in the USA. It became Craig's mission to prevent wrongful convictions and get innocent people released from prison. He managed to get the funding to set up a conviction integrity unit to review old cases to check for evidence of innocence. Many prisoners have since been released and other counties are now using Craig's idea to create similar units.

CLAUDIA JONES

BORN:
21 February 1915 –
died 24 December
1964

NATIONALITY:
Trinidadian

OCCUPATION:
Journalist and
activist

There was something special about Claudia Jones. Like superheroes, Claudia found a cause and fought for it.

In 1924, Claudia's whole family moved from Trinidad in the Caribbean to New York, USA. Life wasn't easy, especially after her father lost his job. As a young black person growing up in America, Claudia realised how difficult it was for her to succeed, especially because she was a woman. She became a political journalist and joined the Young Communist League of America.

During the 1940s and 50s, Claudia was arrested three times by the FBI (the Federal Bureau of Investigation) and was put into prison, where her health suffered. On her release from prison, the USA deported her to Britain where she founded one of the first black newspapers, the *West Indian Gazette*, to inform and connect Britain's growing Afro-Caribbean community.

Claudia also started an indoor Caribbean carnival, held for the first time in London in 1959. After her death, this became the famous Notting Hill Carnival, one of the biggest street festivals in the world.

SARAN KABA JONES

Saran Kaba Jones and her family fled war-torn Liberia when she was eight years old. She spent the next twenty years living wherever her ambassador father's job took the family. When Saran returned to Liberia when she was 26, she was shocked by what she saw.

The civil war had destroyed the country. Most people had no access to clean water, drains, electricity, hospitals or schools. Saran was desperate to help. She founded the organisation Fund a Child's Education (FACE) Africa as a way to rebuild the country through education. She soon changed the plan when she realised that the real problem was a lack of clean drinking water. Children weren't going to school because they were either ill, often because of drinking unclean water, or they didn't have time for school because they had to spend hours walking to rivers to fetch water.

BORN:
12 June 1982

NATIONALITY:
Liberian

OCCUPATION:
Social entrepreneur

Saran refocused FACE Africa to supply safe, clean water supplies to communities in Liberia. To date, it has completed over 50 community projects, bringing water to over 25,000 people.

PAUL STEPHENSON

BORN:
6 May 1937

NATIONALITY:
British

OCCUPATION:
Youth worker and activist

Eighteen-year-old Guy Bailey had arrived on time for his interview to be a bus driver with the Bristol Omnibus Company. He was told that all the positions had been filled. How? One of his white friends had got a job there just the day before. This was the tipping point that ignited the Bristol bus boycott in Britain in 1963.

Paul Stephenson, a youth worker who knew Guy, had followed the year-long Montgomery bus boycott in the USA (see page 28). He was expecting something similar to happen in Britain one day and was prepared to act. He contacted the local newspapers and radio stations and urged them to attend his press conference. There he called for the people of Bristol to boycott the buses until the bus company agreed to change its policy, and employ black and white people for the same types of job.

The Bristol bus boycott lasted for 60 days, until the bus company backed down. It helped to pave the way for the UK Race Relations Act of 1965 that made it illegal to treat someone differently or unfairly because of the colour of their skin.

"Thanks to Paul's courage, principles and determination, Britain is a more open and tolerant place today."

GLOSSARY

Aboriginal Australian the earliest inhabitants of Australia

Afro-Caribbean someone who comes, or whose family comes, from the Caribbean, and whose ancestors originally came from Africa

ambassador someone who lives in a foreign country and is a senior representative of his or her own government

American Civil War (1861–1865) the war fought between the northern and southern states of the USA, triggered by opposing views about whether slavery should continue or not

asylum seeker someone who has been forced to leave their own country because they are in danger and arrives in another country in order to ask for the right to live there safely

black nationalism a political movement particularly strong in the 1960s and early 1970s in the USA. It wanted black Americans to live in their own independent country

boycott refuse to use or buy something as a protest

British Empire the countries ruled by Britain from the late 15th century until many gained independence in the first half of the 20th century. Many became colonies – see below

campaigner a person who takes part in a campaign, working for change

civil rights the rights of a person to fair and equal treatment, regardless of their race, religion or gender

civil war when war breaks out between groups of people in the same country

clergyman a religious leader, especially in the Christian church (also called pastor or minister)

climate change changes in the Earth's usual weather patterns

colony a country or area ruled by another more powerful country

communist someone who belongs to a political movement that believes in a system where the government controls and distributes all resources

conservation working to protect the natural world and all the wildlife that lives in it

conviction finding someone guilty of a crime in a court of law

deport to force someone to leave a country

diplomat someone who represents their country abroad

discrimination treating someone, or a group of people, unfairly

FBI short for the Federal Bureau of Investigation in the USA – the government department that is mainly concerned with national security

genocide the murder of a large group of people

human rights the rights that people are born with, especially the right to be treated fairly and to be able to live the life they choose

immigrant someone who was not born in the country they have made their home

Islam the religion of Muslims

lynching killing someone illegally, often carried out by a group of people

missionary a religious person who devotes their life to spreading the word of their faith

multicultural a society made up of people of many different religions, languages, cultures and races

Nation of Islam an African-American organisation founded in 1930 in the USA that combined elements of Islam with black nationalist ideas

Nobel Peace Prize an international prize awarded to recognise someone's work towards world peace

nuclear weapons very powerful and deadly explosives powered by nuclear reactions

pass laws laws used to control the movement of black, Indian or other non-white people in South Africa

racism the belief that different races possess different characteristics in order to say that one is superior to the other – and the prejudice, discrimination and poor treatment of people against whom racism is directed

rally a group of people who gather together, often to support a particular cause or political party

rights see human rights/civil rights

scholarship a grant or payment to help support a student's education, awarded on the basis of them standing out from others in their level of education or some other talent

segregation in the USA during the 19th and 20th centuries, the system of separating white Americans from black Americans in order to deny them equal opportunities in education, health, housing and other areas

senate one of the groups of people who make the laws of the country

slavery the condition of some people owning other people

tear gas a gas that makes your eyes stream

terrorism the use of violent action in order to try to force a government to act

tribal describing a group of people who share the same language, culture or religion and live in a particular area

United Nations an organisation of many countries which aims to solve the problems of the world in a peaceful way

FURTHER INFORMATION

Books

Civil Rights Then & Now: A Timeline of the Fight for Equality in America by Kristina Brooke-Daniele (Wendybird Press, 2018)
Black History Matters by Robin Walker (Franklin Watts, 2019)
Young, Gifted and Black by Jamia Wilson and Andrea Pippins (Wide-Eyed Editions, 2018)

Websites and videos

Watch **Martin Luther King**'s inspiring 'I have a dream' speech at www.youtube.com/watch?v=vP4iY1TtS3s

Find out more about **Rosa Parks** at: www.blackhistorymonth.org.uk/article/section/civil-rights-movement/rosa-parks-the-mother-of-the-modern-day-civil-rights-movement/
Discover more about Harriet Tubman at the **Harriet Tubman Museum** website: www.tubmanmuseum.com

The website addresses (URLs) included in this book were valid at the time of going to press. However, it is possible that contents or addresses may have changed since the publication of this book. No responsibility for any such changes can be accepted by either the author or the Publisher.

QUOTE SOURCES

Kofi Annan: p.4: 'I remain convinced…' United Nations Foundation, 'A Tribute to Kofi Annan', October 15, 2018. Digital; p.5: 'There can be no doubt…' www.UN.Org. **Harriet Tubman**: p.8: 'When I found…' Hopkins-Bradford, Sarah 'Scenes in the Life of Harriet Tubman', 1869; p.11: 'I was a conductor…' www.harriet-tubman.org. **Lowitja O'Donoghue**: p.12: 'I always thought…' NFSA Digital Learning, 'Lowitja O'Donoghue-Reunion', Digital. **Nelson Mandela:** p.17: 'There are many people…' Belarus, UN 'Nelson Mandela's Life Story,' July 13, 2011; p.19: 'We shall build…' https://www.africa.upenn.edu/Articles_Gen/Inaugural_Speech_17984.html 10 May 1994. **Umra Omar:** p.21: 'It was…' Torgan, Allie, 'Group Braves Danger Delivering Health Care to Rural Kenya', CNN, February 13, 2017. Digital; p.21: 'We put together…' 'Group Braves Danger Delivering Health Care to Rural Kenya', CNN, February 13, 2017. Digital. **Patrisse Cullors**: 'When you're bringing…' VProDocumentary, 'The Rise of Black Lives Matter' 2016, December 4, 2016. Digital. **Rosa Parks**: p.28: 'I was tired…' Manufacturing Intellect, Rosa Parks Interview (1995) August 26, 2017. Digital. **Dr Martin Luther King**: p.31: 'The events in Birmingham…' Afriwarraw, 'Malcolm X and Martin Luther King, Jr. Face to Face in Unity!' January 4, 2018. Digital. **Barack Obama**: p.37: 'In no other country…' Obama, Barack from keynote speech to Democratic National Congress, 27 July, 2004; p.39: "In no other…' Obama, Barack from Health Care Address to Congress, 9 September, 2009. **Paul Stephenson**: p.58: 'Thanks to Paul…' Pride of Britain judges, https://www.prideofbritain.com/component/k2/dr-paul-stephenson-obe.

INDEX

First published in Great Britain
in 2020 by Wayland
Copyright © Hodder and Stoughton, 2020
All rights reserved

Series editor: Julia Bird
Designer: Peter Scoulding
Artist: Chellie Carroll

ISBN: 978 1 5263 1378 2

Wayland
An imprint of Hachette Children's Group
Part of Hodder and Stoughton
Carmelite House
50 Victoria Embankment
London EC4Y 0DZ

An Hachette UK Company
www.hachette.co.uk
www.hachettechildrens.co.uk

Printed in Dubai

MIX
Paper from
responsible sources
FSC® C104740